# Australian Shepherds
## at Work

### Sabrina Lakes

xist Publishing

# Check out all of the books in the Paws and Pastures Series

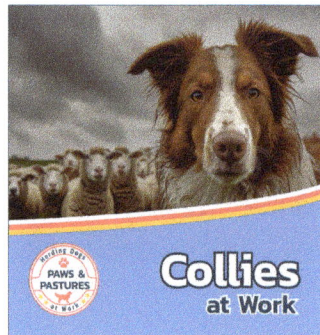

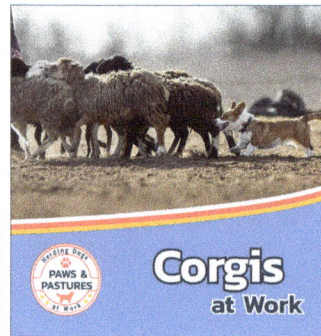

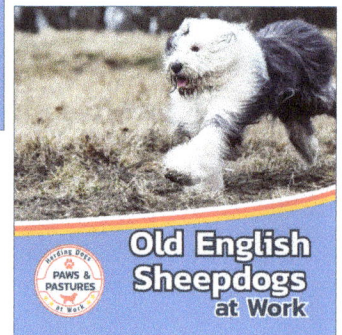

Australian Shepherds at Work

Collies at Work

Corgis at Work

Old English Sheepdogs at Work

Published in the United States by Xist Publishing
www.xistpublishing.com
© 2025 Copyright Xist Publishing

First Edition
Hardcover ISBN: 978-1-5324-5539-1
Paperback ISBN: 978-1-5324-5540-7
eISBN: 978-1-5324-5538-4

PUBLISHED IN TEXAS

# Table of Contents

# Introduction to Australian Shepherds

Australian Shepherds are medium-sized dogs. They have a lot of energy and love to work. They come from the United States, not Australia! Farmers use them to help with animals. Australian Shepherds are smart and friendly. They enjoy playing and learning new tricks.

# Fun Facts About Australian Shepherds

Australian Shepherds are very active. They can run and jump very well. Their fur can be many colors like black, blue, and red. Australian Shepherds have bright eyes that can be blue, brown, or even one of each. They are great helpers and love to be with people.

# What is Herding?

Herding means guiding animals like sheep or cows. Australian Shepherds help farmers keep animals in groups. They move the animals to new places. This job is very important on farms.

# Why are Australian Shepherds Great Herders?

Australian Shepherds are great herders because they are smart and quick. They learn commands easily and love to work. Their strong bodies help them run and turn quickly. Australian Shepherds are also very brave and can handle big animals. They are always ready to help!

# Training an Australian Shepherd

Training an Australian Shepherd is exciting and rewarding. Start with basic commands like "sit" and "stay." Give treats to reward good behavior. Be patient and positive. Australian Shepherds love to please their owners and enjoy learning new skills.

# Games to Help Australian Shepherds Learn

Games make training enjoyable for Australian Shepherds. Play fetch to teach them to come back quickly. Hide treats for them to find using their strong noses. Another fun game is herding a ball, which helps them practice herding skills in a playful way.

# A Day in the Life of a Working Australian Shepherd

Australian Shepherds begin their day full of energy. After breakfast, they get ready to work. They help the farmer by guiding the animals out to the fields. Australian Shepherds are always eager to start their day.

## Working with the Animals

Throughout the day, Australian Shepherds work hard. They keep the animals together and make sure they stay safe. They move quickly and use their barks to guide the animals. Australian Shepherds are excellent at their job and enjoy every moment of it.

## Caring for an Australian Shepherd

Australian Shepherds need nutritious food to stay healthy and strong. They eat balanced meals twice a day. Brushing their fur regularly keeps it clean and shiny. Trimming their nails helps them run and play without discomfort.

# Keeping Your Australian Shepherd Healthy

Australian Shepherds need daily exercise to stay fit. Walks, playtime, and working keep them happy. Regular check-ups at the vet ensure they stay in good health. Australian Shepherds love being active and thrive when they have plenty to do.

# Australian Shepherds at Rest

After a busy day, Australian Shepherds need to rest. They enjoy napping in cozy spots to recharge. Resting helps them get ready for another day of work and play. They also like cuddling with their family members.

# Fun Activities for Australian Shepherds

Even when resting, Australian Shepherds love to play. They enjoy toys that squeak or bounce. Puzzle toys challenge their minds and keep them entertained. Spending time with their family is their favorite activity of all.

# Glossary

**Balanced Meals**  Nutritious food that keeps dogs healthy and strong.

**Commands**  Words or signals used to tell a dog what to do, like "sit" or "stay."

**Exercise**  Activities like walking or playing that help keep a dog strong and fit.

**Grooming**  Taking care of a dog's fur and nails to keep them clean and healthy.

**Herding**  Guiding and moving animals like sheep or cows.

**Nutritious**  Food that is healthy and good for growth and strength.

**Puzzle Toys**  Toys that challenge a dog's mind and keep them entertained.

**Recharge**  Resting to get energy back after working or playing.

**Treats**  Special food given to dogs as a reward for good behavior.

# Index

# Keyword List

| Nouns | Verbs | Adjectives | Adverbs |
|---|---|---|---|
| animals | are | active | easily |
| Australia | be | Australian | excellent |
| ball | can | brave | quickly |
| behavior | come | friendly | safe |
| bodies | find | good | very |
| breakfast | give | great | well |
| colors | guide | important | |
| commands | have | playful | |
| cows | help | safe | |
| dogs | is | strong | |
| energy | jump | | |
| eyes | keep | | |
| farm | move | | |
| farmers | play | | |
| fields | run | | |
| fur | start | | |
| Shepherds | stay | | |
| work | use | | |

Herding Dogs

PAWS &
PASTURES

at Work

www.ingramcontent.com/pod-product-compliance
Lightning Source LLC
LaVergne TN
LVHW070835080426
835508LV00031B/3467